get on!

Englisch mit Spaß!

Übungen, Rätsel, Spiele und Lerntipps für Anfänger

Manfred Bojes
Illustrationen von Rolf Vogt

1

arsEdition

1. Auflage 2002

Gesamtgestaltung: Kathi Kappler,
Johann Rüttinger, Rolf Vogt
Redaktion: Heike John
Sprachliche Beratung: Helen van Rensburg
ISBN 3-7607-5842-8

www.arsedition.de

Contents

3

Ein paar Tipps vorweg

Für viele der folgenden Übungen und Rätsel brauchst du ein Blatt Papier und einen Stift, damit du die Lösungen notieren kannst. Zur Kontrolle finden sich alle Auflösungen jeweils am Kapitelende.

Die Übungen bauen nicht zwingend aufeinander auf, d.h. du musst sie nicht alle der Reihe nach lösen, sondern kannst von Kapitel zu Kapitel springen. Im Anhang findest du eine Übersicht über die behandelten grammatischen Themen.

Und nun viel Spaß!

The Cool Family

Billy Cool

Carla Cool

Lilly Cool

Bobby Cool

Molly MacMuff

Maxi MacMuff

Bolly Cool

Holly Cool

Ben MacMuff

This is the Cool family:

Mr Bobby Cool, Mrs Lilly Cool, their daughter Holly and their son Bolly. Billy Cool is Holly's and Bolly's grandfather, and Carla Cool is their grandmother. Mr MacMuff and Mrs MacMuff are their uncle and aunt. Ben MacMuff is their cousin.

Do you know the Cool family tree?
Find out what is right or wrong. Note »yes« or »no«.

> **Example:**
> Mr Cool: »Holly is my daughter.« **Yes.**

1. Holly and Bolly: »Ben is our uncle.«
2. Ben: »Bolly is my son.«
3. Bolly: »Holly is my sister.«
4. Ben: »Lilly Cool is my aunt.«
5. Bolly: »This is Holly, and Carla is her mother.«
6. Holly: »Hey, Ben, my father is your uncle.«
7. Ben: »Here is Bolly, and Lilly is his mother.«
8. Billy: »Look at Bolly and Holly: Ben is their brother.«
9. Bobby: »Carla is Ben's grandmother.«

Scrambled words

Can you find the family words?
Write them on a paper, please.

1. nuta
2. neluc
3. dranghetfar
4. nos
5. haudregt
6. restis
7. rethorb
8. sucino
9. hertmo
10. tremardhong
11. hertfa

A puzzle for clever kids only:
Mr Cool is Mrs Cool's subhand,
and Mrs Cool is Mr Cool's iwef.

The »Yes or No Game«

Kennst du das Yes-or-no-Spiel?

Du brauchst nur zwei Stühle und mindestens zwei Mitspieler dazu. Die Stühle stellst du in einem Abstand von einigen Metern voneinander auf, sodass ihre Sitzflächen zur Mitte zeigen.

Den einen Stuhl nennt ihr »Yes-Chair«, den anderen »No-Chair«. In der Mitte zwischen beiden Stühlen stellen sich nun zwei Mitspieler Rücken an Rücken auf.

Ein Spielleiter sagt anschließend einen Satz auf Englisch. War er richtig, müssen die Spieler versuchen, schnell den »Yes-Chair« zu erreichen oder umgekehrt. Der Schnellere erreicht ihn und bleibt im Spiel. Der Zweite wird durch einen anderen ersetzt.

Gute Sätze sind Aussagen über die Familien der Mitspieler oder die Beispiele von Seite 6.

Weitere Möglichkeiten:

Ben is Bolly's father. – Mr MacMuff is Ben's father.
Bill is Carla's grandmother. – Ben is Holly's cousin.
Holly is Ben's aunt. – Billy is Ben's uncle.

Who is that?

Find the missing words and write them down.

Who is who? Look for help on page 5.

answers on page 16

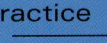

1. Who is that?
   That is ❶ ....
   She is Bolly's ❷ ....

2. Who is ❸ .... ?
   That ❹ ....
   She is Holly's and Bolly's ❺ ....

3. Who ❻ .... ?
   That ❼ ....
   She is Holly's and Bolly's ❽ ....

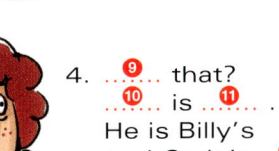

4. ❾ .... that?
   ❿ .... is ⓫ ....
   He is Billy's and Carla's ⓬ ....

5. ⓭ .... ?
   That ⓮ ....
   He is Holly's ⓯ ....

Holly's and Bolly's friends

Who? Where? How old?
Find the missing questions or answers.

Name: **Molly Vanolly**
From: London
Age: 13

Who is that?
❶ ....
❷ .... ?
She is from London.
How old is she?
❸ ....

Name: **Tony Ticket**
From: Tottenham
Age: 10

❹ .... ?
That is ❺ ....
Where is he ❻ .... ?
❼ ....
❽ .... ?
He ❾ ....

Name: **Barney Basket**
From: Manchester
Age: 12

❿ .... ?
⓫ ....
⓬ .... ?
⓭ ....
⓮ .... ?
⓯ ....

Lerntipp: *who* und *where*

Wir deutschen Sprecher haben immer wieder Schwierigkeiten, die beiden englischen Fragewörter **who** und **where** auseinander zu halten.

Das liegt daran, dass die Aussprache und auch die Schreibweise der englischen Wörter in der deutschen Sprache genau das Umgekehrte ausdrücken wie im Englischen.

Where bedeutet also »wo« und **who** heißt »wer«!

Anders gesagt:

who = wer
where = wo

Am allerbesten kann man sich das aber mit diesem Reim merken:

who heißt *wer* und *where* heißt *wo*, das weiß doch jeder Englisch-Floh!

Dogs

Put in the missing words.
my – your – his – her – our – their

Molly Vanolly:
Hi, Holly and Bolly,
are ...①... mother and father here?

Holly:
No, but ...②... new dogs are here, look.
...③... names are Pit and Pat.

Molly Vanolly:
Hey, nice names.
...④... dog's name is Mixy.

Bolly:
Pit is a boy.
...⑤... hobby is barking, listen.
Pat is a girl.
...⑥... hobby is eating dog food, look.

A family tree

Wenn du Spaß am Malen und Zeichnen hast, kannst du nun entweder deinen eigenen Stammbaum aufmalen oder dir einen fantastischen Familienstammbaum mit lustigen englischen Namen ausdenken und aufzeichnen. Anregungen für solche Namen bietet dir ein englisch-deutsches Wörterbuch, in dem du auch eine Liste mit englischen Vornamen findest. Hier siehst du ein Beispiel, wie der **family tree** aussehen könnte. Sicher hast du auch eigene Ideen, wie man ihn ansprechend gestalten könnte. Anschließend kannst du ihn nicht nur deiner Familie, sondern auch deinen Freunden und deiner Englischlehrerin oder deinem Englischlehrer zeigen.

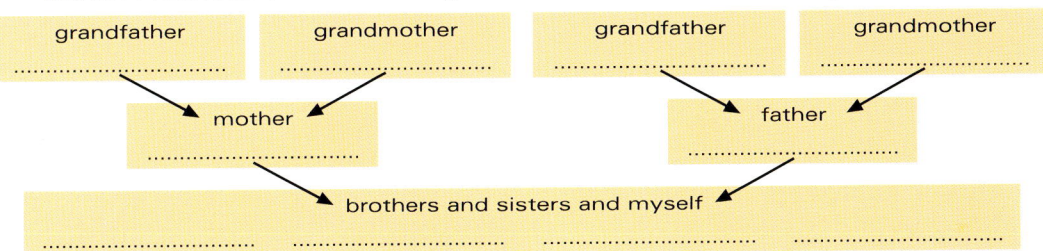

Natürlich können auch noch Verzweigungen mit Onkeln und Tanten, Cousins und Cousinen etc. erscheinen.

The Cool family and their friends

Put in the missing words.
I – you – he – she – it – we – you – they

1. **Bobby and Lilly**
   are English.
   ...①... are Ben's
   uncle and aunt.

2. **Tony Ticket**
   is from Tottenham.
   ...②... is 10.

3. What is **Pat's** hobby?
   ...③... is eating dog food.

4. Where is
   Molly Vanolly from?
   ...④... is from London.

5. **Carla Cool:**
   » ...⑤... am Ben's
   grandmother.«

6. **Holly and Bolly:**
   » ...⑥... are Ben's cousins.«

7. **Bolly:** »Hi, Barney, ...⑦... are
   our good friend.«

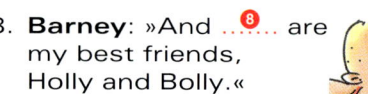

8. **Barney**: »And ...⑧... are
   my best friends,
   Holly and Bolly.«

More questions

Can you find the right answers?

1. **Is this a dog?**
   a) Yes, it is.
   b) No, it isn't.
   c) Yes, she is.
   d) No, he isn't.

2. **Are they skaters?**
   a) No, they aren't.
   b) Yes, he is.
   c) No, it isn't.
   d) Yes, they are.

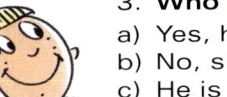

3. **Who is he?**
   a) Yes, he is.
   b) No, she isn't
   c) He is Ben.
   d) Ben is a boy.

4. **Is Bolly a girl?**
   a) No, she isn't.
   b) Yes, he is.
   c) Yes, they are.
   d) No, he isn't.

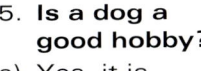

5. **Is a dog a good hobby?**
   a) Yes, it is.
   b) No, they aren't.
   c) Yes, he is.
   d) No, she isn't.

Answers Chapter 1: Family

p. 6:   1. No, 2. No, 3. Yes, 4. Yes, 5. No, 6. Yes, 7. Yes, 8. No, 9. Yes

p. 7:   1. aunt, 2. uncle, 3. grandfather, 4. son, 5. daughter,
6. sister, 7. brother, 8. cousin, 9. mother, 10. grandmother, 11. father
For clever kids: husband – wife

p. 9:   1. Holly, 2. sister, 3. that, 4. is Carla, 5. grandmother, 6. is that,
7. is Mrs MacMuff, 8. aunt, 9. Who is, 10. That, 11. Bobby Cool, 12. son, 13. Who is that,
14. is Bolly, 15. brother

p. 10:   1. That is Molly Vanolly. – 2. Where is she from? – 3. She is 13/thirteen. – 4. Who is that? –
5. Tony Ticket – 6. from – 7. He is from Tottenham. – 8. How old is he? – 9. is 10/ten –
10. Who is that? – 11. That is Barney Basket. – 12. Where is he from? – 13. He is from Manchester. –
14. How old is he? – 15. He is 12/twelve.

p. 12:   1. your, 2. our, 3. Their, 4. My, 5. His, 6. Her

p. 14:   1. They, 2. He, 3. It, 4. She, 5. I, 6. We, 7. you, 8. you

p. 15:   1. b), 2. d), 3. c), 4. d), 5. a)

Four Friends

Holly has three friends: **Dicky, Nelly and Slimmy.**

Dicky has very short brown hair and he is younger than Nelly and Slimmy – and he is the shortest, look!

Nelly and Slimmy aren't from London, they are from York.
Slimmy is older than Nelly and Holly.
He is the oldest of Holly's friends and he has the longest hair.

The four friends have a hobby.
Their hobby is making funny interviews.

Holly's friends

Do you remember how Holly's friends look and what they like to do?

Can you put the sentences together?
Write them on a paper, please.

1. Dicky's hair
2. Dicky is
3. Nelly and Slimmy
4. Slimmy is
5. Slimmy has
6. The four friends
7. Their hobby

a) the oldest.
b) is making funny interviews.
c) are from York.
d) the longest hair.
e) is short and brown.
f) have a hobby.
g) the shortest.

A funny interview

Can you find Slimmy's answers?

Friends
practice

answers on page 28

19

Example

Holly: Is Nelly your sister, Slimmy?   Slimmy: No, she isn't.

1. Are you at a monster school?   No, ❶ ....
2. Is Nelly your best friend?   Yes, ❷ ....
3. Are you and Dicky brothers?   No, ❸ ....
4. Are you 14?   Yes, ❹ ....
5. Are the girls here nicer than in New York?   Yes, ❺ ....
6. Is Dicky a punk?   No, ❻ ....
7. Am I a good friend?   Yes, ❼ ....
8. Has Dicky long purple hair?   No, ❽ ....
9. Have we all funny faces?   Yes, ❾ .... – I hope so!
10. Is this interview terrible?   No, ❿ .... But it's too long. It's longer than my English homework.

Opposites

Can you find the opposites?

good player

bad player

1. the oldest	a) loser
2. good	b) daughter
3. smaller than	c) the shortest
4. put on	d) colder than
5. black	e) boring
6. the longest	f) white
7. warmer than	g) the unhappiest
8. interesting	h) bigger than
9. son	i) uncle
10. winner	j) stop
11. aunt	k) the youngest
12. cleaner than	l) take off
13. the happiest	m) bad
14. start	n) dirtier than

»Ready – Steady – Go!«

Bei diesem Spiel kommt es auf Schnelligkeit und Vokabelwissen an.

Du brauchst dafür einen Spielleiter und mindestens zwei Teams, die gegeneinander spielen. Zu jedem Team sollten zwei Mitspieler gehören. Zunächst werden alle Teams bis auf Team 1 hinausgeschickt. Team 1 wird die Aufgabe gestellt.

Beispiel:
»Tell me what you can eat and drink.«

Ab jetzt läuft die Zeit, z. B. eine Minute. Die Teammitglieder müssen nun abwechselnd auf Englisch Sachen nennen, die man essen oder trinken kann. Jedes richtige Wort ergibt einen Punkt. Nach einer Minute wird das zweite Team hereingerufen und erhält dieselbe Aufgabe. Das Team mit den meisten Punkten gewinnt.

Hier sind einige gute Aufgaben für das Spiel:

What can you see in this room?
What can you do in the holidays?
Tell me all the things you can do! (Verbs)
What can you see in a city centre – at a swimming pool – in a supermarket – in a school?

E-mail to a friend

**The words in the box
are missing.**

Put them in, please.

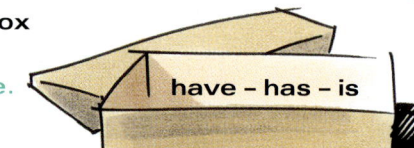

have – has – is

Hi Freddy,
my old friend in York,

I **❶** a new friend here in London. She **❷** twelve, and her name **❸**
interesting: it **❹** Holly. She **❺** a brother. His name **❻** Bolly. That's
funny, isn't it? He **❼** nice, too. We **❽** a hobby together: making interviews. Oh, Freddy can you give me a tip? I **❾** a message for Holly.
The message **❿** :

I ❤ YOU!

What do you think, can I tell her?????

Yours
Slimmy
P.S.: Please write soon!!!!

Comparisons

Can you put the sentences in the right order?

1. colder / than / January / July. / is

2. as / as / not / is / old / Nelly. / Dicky

3. a VW Golf. / A Ferrari / faster / is / than

4. the shortest / February / month. / is

5. Budgies / buses. / are / as / not / as / big

6. Speaking English / writing English. / than easier / is

7. books. / Comics / funnier / than / are

8. and August / months. / are / July the warmest

Lerntipp: *to be*

Du hast sicher wie selbstverständlich und sehr rasch gelernt, wann man I am, you are, he/she/it is, we are, they are benutzt.

Die Wörter **am**, **is**, **are** sind alle Formen des Wortes **be** = sein, obwohl man ihnen das auf den ersten Blick wirklich nicht ansieht.

Aber mal ehrlich: Sieht man in unserer deutschen Sprache den Wörtern »bin« oder »ist«, »sind« oder »seid« auf den ersten Blick an, dass sie Formen von »sein« sind? Du kannst dir die Formen von **be** am besten so wie Vokabeln einprägen.

Also:

I am	=	**ich bin**
you are	=	**du bist**
he, she, it is	=	**er, sie, es ist**
we are	=	**wir sind**
you are	=	**ihr seid**
they are	=	**sie sind**

You are gibt es zweimal: Es kann »**du bist**« oder »**ihr seid**« heißen. Welche der beiden Bedeutungen gerade gemeint ist, kannst du herausfinden, wenn du dir den ganzen Satz genau durchliest oder anhörst.

Alles klar? Dann kannst du dir diesen hilfreichen Spruch merken:

Jetzt ists mir klar wie nie, am – is – are sind von to be.
Du bist, ihr seid, auch das ist klar, heißen beide nur: you are!

Odd man out

Can you find the odd man out?

1. blue / green / old / brown
2. mother / teacher / cousin / father
3. run / stand / sit / great
4. go / who / what / where
5. I / he / they / bye
6. old / new / class / great
7. pencil / ruler / yellow / rubber
8. put / in / on / behind
9. shop / van / road / grandmother
10. school / terrible / house / shop
11. no / nine / eight / three
12. cupboard / table / door / map

Du kannst dir auch selbst solche Rätsel ausdenken
und sie dann in der Schule oder deinen Freunden vorstellen.

A poster

Can you make a poster of your friends?

Wie wärs mit einem englischen Poster über deine Freunde? Du versuchst, einen oder mehrere von ihnen zu malen und einige Aussagen über sie auf Englisch zu machen, die du ebenfalls auf dem Poster unterbringst.

Hier ein Beispiel:

Ihr werdet viel Spaß haben, wenn ihr euch gegenseitig malt und eure Poster anschließend austauscht!

This is Chris.
He is eleven.
He is my friend.
He is funny.
His hobby is eating ice cream!
We are from Frankfurt.
Chris has a little sister.
Her name is Sonja.

Another funny interview

Put in the missing words in the questions.

1. Hey, Dicky, ...①... you 20?

No, I'm not 20, I'm 9.

2. ...②... your hobby eating ice cream?

Yes, eating ice cream is my hobby.

3. ...③... your mother younger than you?

No, she is older, of course.

4. ...④... she two children?

No, she has one kid. Just me!

5. ...⑤... you a girl friend?

Yes, of course. Her name is Madonna!

6. Madonna? She ...⑥... older than you!

Well, I like big girls. But I hate silly questions.

7. Hey, Dicky, wait, please!

Bye bye!!

   ...⑦... you angry now?

....

Answers Chapter 2: Friends

p. 18: 1. e), 2. g), 3. c), 4. a), 5. d), 6. f), 7. b)

p. 19: 1. I'm not − 2. she is − 3. we aren't − 4. I am − 5. they are −
6. he isn't − 7. you are − 8. he hasn't − 9. we have − 10. it isn't

p. 20: 2. m), 3. h), 4. l), 5. f), 6. c), 7. d), 8. e), 9. b), 10. a), 11. i), 12. n), 13. g), 14. j)

p. 22: 1. have, 2. is, 3. is, 4. is, 5. has, 6. is, 7. is, 8. have, 9. have, 10. is

p. 23: 1. January is colder than July. − 2. Dicky is not as old as Nelly. −
3. A Ferrari is faster than a VW Golf. − 4. February is the shortest month. −
5. Budgies are not as big as buses. − 6. Speaking English is easier than writing English. −
7. Comics are funnier than books. − 8. July and August are the warmest months.

p. 25: 1. old, 2. teacher, 3. great, 4. go, 5. bye, 6. class, 7. yellow, 8. put, 9. grandmother,
10. terrible, 11. no, 12. map

p. 27: 1. are, 2. Is, 3. Is, 4. Has, 5. Have, 6. is, 7. Are

Freddy from York

Freddy Footstep is from York. His parents have got a flat in Fulford near the park.

Fulford is not in the city centre, but there is a post office, a supermarket, a school and there are snack bars and shops. A small village in a big town!

Freddy has got a nice room. It has got a big window and a new green carpet. There is a white table and a yellow bed. There are two brown cupboards, two red chairs and three colour posters.

Freddy can't see the school from his window, but he can see the park. Freddy says: »My room is my castle. It's great!«

Can you remember?

Here are 12 sentences about Freddy and Fulford. They are all wrong.

Can you make them right?

1. His parents have got a house.
2. It is near the swimming pool.
3. There is a doctor's office in Fulford.
4. There are four supermarkets.
5. There are dance bars.
6. Freddy has got a terrible room.
7. It has got an old grey carpet.
8. There is a purple table and an orange bed.
9. Freddy has got three black cupboards.
10. He has got four blue chairs.
11. There are no posters in his room.
12. Freddy can see a castle from his window.

Mix a colour

Mix the colours and find the new colour.

Example:

| blue | + | red | = | purple |

1. red + yellow = ?
2. blue + yellow = ?
3. grey – white = ?
4. green – yellow = ?
5. purple – blue = ?
6. grey – black = ?
7. black + white = ?
8. orange – red = ?
9. green – blue = ?

Freddy's room

Look at the picture and put the sentences together. Write them down on a paper.

a) 1. green / in / room. / Freddy's / is / There / a / carpet /
2. the / on / books / three / are / table. / There
3. cat / room. / his / in / is / a / There
4. in / are / two / Freddy's / There / teddies / bed.

b) 1. parents / flat / haven't / city centre. / a / got / Freddy's / the / in
2. room / got / window. / Freddy's / a / has / big
3. got / black / cat. / has / a / white / Freddy / and
4. Freddy / a / got / cream / hasn't / table.

c) Can you answer the questions with short answers?

1. Has Freddy got a dog?
2. Has the room got a cream door?
3. Have Freddy's parents got a house in a park?
4. Has his cat got an orange basket?

Lerntipp: Vokabeln lernen

Vokabeln lernen – aber wie?

Vokabeln lernen bereitet vielen Kindern Schwierigkeiten.
Kein Wunder – es ist manchmal wirklich nicht leicht!

Man kann sich die Sache aber doch leichter machen, wenn man
weiß, wie man neue Wörter schnell und wirkungsvoll lernen kann.

Hierfür gibt es ein paar goldene Regeln, die man befolgen sollte.
Sie stellen eine große Hilfe dar:

1. Suche dir einen Raum für dich allein.

2. Stelle Fernseher und Musik unbedingt ab.

3. Lerne nicht länger als 10 Minuten auf einmal.

4. Nimm dir nicht mehr als 12 Vokabeln auf
   einmal vor.

5. Lerne lieber fünfmal in der Woche für 10 Minuten
   als einmal pro Woche eine Stunde lang.

Town words

Look at the pictures and find out the town words.

1. ruchch
2. olosch
3. sub post
4. laclxob
5. hops
6. putsmerrake
7. ytci rentec
8. krap
9. stop ficefo
10. lageliv
11. wotn
12. etrets
13. cilepo nostita
14. ixat
15. ikeb
16. rac

Can or can't?

Put in: he, she, they + can / can't.

1. Can Emily draw?   Yes,  ....
2. Can she speak German?   No, ...

3. Can Pinky and Punky write?   Yes, ...
4. Can they make hamburgers?   No, ...

5. Can Barky spell?   No, ...
6. Can he make dog music?   Yes, ...

7. Can Pussy read comics?   No, ...
8. Can she listen to music?   Yes,  ....

9. Can Boy-boy play football?   Yes, ...
10. Can he see Pussy?   No,  ....

Picturequick

Bei diesem Spiel kommt es darauf an, in möglichst kurzer Zeit möglichst viele Gegenstände, die ein Mitspieler zeichnet, mit dem englischen Begriff zu erraten.

Benötigt werden ein Spielleiter, mindestens zwei Mannschaften mit je zwei oder mehr Mitspielern, eine Malfläche und mehrere Blätter Papier.

Zunächst müssen alle Teams den Raum verlassen und der Spielleiter schreibt etwa 10 bis 20 englische Wörter auf verschiedene Blätter oder Kärtchen.

Das erste Team wird hereingerufen. Der Spielleiter zeigt dem Zeichner aus dem Team den ersten Begriff. Der zeichnet den Begriff möglichst rasch auf und seine Mitspieler versuchen ihn zu erraten. Danach wird dem Zeichner der nächste Begriff gezeigt, bis die vereinbarte Zeit vorbei ist. Der Spielleiter notiert die Anzahl der erratenen Begriffe und ruft die nächste Mannschaft herein.

Das Team, das in der vorgegebenen Zeit die meisten Wörter herausgefunden hat, gewinnt.

Prima Begriffe für dieses Spiel findest du auf Seite 34 bei den **town words**!

Susy Softwood

Put the sentences together.

Hi I'M SUSY!

Susy Softwood
is Freddy's friend.

1. have got a /   / in Fulford. / The Softwoods

2. has got a / small room / in the /   / Susy

3. What / in her room? / has she got

4. She has got / poster / a funny / CD-player. / and a new

5. in their garden. / The Softwoods / a big round / have got /

6. have got a /   / They

7. Dinah, the /   / is in the garden /   / with a big blue

8. is her hobby. / the big blue /   / Playing with

9.   / you got / a / , too? / Have

The detective game

Für dieses Spiel brauchst du mindestens
einen Mitspieler.

Du denkst dir zuerst aus, in welche Person du schlüpfen
möchtest. Das kann eine berühmte Person sein, aber auch
eine Freundin, ein Freund oder ein Familienmitglied.

Nachdem du dir überlegt hast, wer du sein willst, müssen die anderen
auf Englisch herausfinden, wer du bist. Dabei können sie z.B. folgende
Fragen stellen, die man alle nur mit **Yes** oder **No** beantworten kann:

Are you a boy / girl / man / woman?
Are you from ...?
Have you got a sister / brother?
Are you 10 / 11 / 12?
Are you a pop star?
Are you a football star?
Are you a tennis star?
Is your hobby ...?
Can you ...?

Man darf nur zweimal direkt nach dem Namen fragen.

My room for a pen pal

Könntest du dein Zimmer aus dem Gedächtnis heraus auf Englisch beschreiben?

Setz dich in einen anderen Raum und schreibe auf, was dir einfällt.

Sätze mit **There is … / There are …** und **I have got …** sind dabei hilfreich. Vergleiche deine Aufzählung danach mit der Wirklichkeit. Hast du etwas Wichtiges vergessen?

Könnte sich eine englischsprachige Brieffreundin oder ein englischsprachiger Brieffreund dein Zimmer vorstellen?

Hast du Lust bekommen, öfter auf Englisch etwas über dich zu erzählen? Dann können dir die folgenden Adressen beim Finden von Brieffreunden helfen:

IYS International Youth Service
PB 125
Fin – 20101 Turku
Finnland

im Internet:
http://www.iys.fi
E-Mail: iys@iys.fi

oder

»Pen Pal International«
im Internet:
http://ppi.searchy.net

Answers Chapter 3: Home town

p. 30: 1. His parents have got a flat. 2. It is near the park. 3. There is a post office in Fulford. 4. There is a/one supermarket. 5. There are snack bars. 6. Freddy has got a nice room. 7. It has got a new green carpet. 8. There is a white table and a yellow bed. 9. He has got two brown cupboards. 10. He has got two red chairs. 11. There are three posters. 12. Freddy can see the park from his window.

p. 31: 1. orange, 2. green, 3. black, 4. blue, 5. red, 6. white, 7. grey, 8. yellow, 9. yellow

p. 32: a) 1. There is a green carpet in Freddy's room. 2. There are three books on the table. 3. There is a cat in his room. 4. There are two teddies in Freddy's bed. b) 1. Freddy's parents haven't got a flat in the city centre. 2. Freddy's room has got a big window. 3. Freddy has got a black and white cat. 4. Freddy hasn't got a cream table. c) 1. No, he hasn't. 2. Yes, it has. 3. No, they haven't. 4. No, it hasn't.

p. 34: 1. church, 2. school, 3. bus stop, 4. callbox, 5. shop, 6. supermarket, 7. city centre, 8. park, 9. post office, 10. village, 11. town, 12. street, 13. police station, 14. taxi, 15. bike, 16. car

p. 35: 1. she can, 2. she can't, 3. they can, 4. they can't, 5. he can't, 6. he can, 7. she can't, 8. she can, 9. he can, 10. he can't

p. 37: 1. The Softwoods have got a house in Fulford. 2. Susy has got a small room in the house. 3. What has she got in her room? 4. She has got a funny poster and a new CD-player. 5. The Softwoods have got a big round table in their garden. 6. They have got a dog. 7. Dinah, the dog, is in the garden with a big blue ball. 8. Playing with the big blue ball is her hobby. 9. Have you got a dog, too?

At the zoo and in the pet shop

Susy Softwood likes wild animals. She often goes to the zoo in York and looks at the lions, tigers, bears, seals, alligators and the dolphins. She loves dolphins very much!

Freddy likes pets.
He sometimes walks to the pet shop and looks at hamsters, budgies, guinea pigs, goldfishs, dogs, cats and rabbits. Rabbits are his favourites!

Can you remember?

Find the right word in every colour box.
Write them on a paper, please.

1. Susy Softwood likes `pets` `dogs` `wild animals` .

2. Freddy likes `pets` `dolphins` `wild animals` .

3. Susy `never` `often` `sometimes` goes to the zoo
   in `York` `Fulford` `New York` .

4. Freddy `always` `never` `sometimes` `rides` `walks` `swims` to the
   pet shop.

5. Susy looks at the `lions` `cats` `guinea pigs` .

6. Freddy looks at the `seals` `budgies` `bears` .

7. Susy `hates` `loves` `eats` `alligators` `dolphins` `tigers` very much.

8. Freddy's favourites are the `goldfish` `rabbits` `dogs` .

Three weeks

Can you find the right words for the sentences?

1. have – buy – meet – say

On Monday I my friend Rocky.
On Thursday I food for my dog.
On Friday I hello to my girlfriend.
On Saturday I a good time with her at the school disco.

2. clean – do – get – look

On Tuesday I a difficult swimming test.
On Wednesday I at lions and tigers at the zoo.
On Saturday I my budgie's cage.
On Sunday I my lunch at the snack bar.

3. make – play – give – see – think

On Monday I : »I like my boyfriend Ricky.«
On Tuesday I a nice picture card for him.
On Saturday I Ricky and I him my picture card.
On Sunday I with my little guinea pig.

Where are they?

Put in: her – him – them

1. a) Where is Susy? – No idea.
   Let's phone ...①... .

   b) Where is Rocky? Can you see ...②... ?

   c) Where is Emmy? I can't see ...③... .

   d) Look, there are our friends. –
   Where? I can't see ...④... .

2. a) Look, there are two white rabbits at
   Mr Green's pet shop. Let's watch ...①... .

   b) Oh, Mr Green must clean their cage.
   Come on, I think we can help ...②... .

   c) Look, there are two sticks in the pool near the dog house. –
   Oh yes, we can take ...③... and play hockey with ...④... .

The animal rap

You can do this rap together with your friends.
You can use instruments or your voices to make
sounds like the animals.

Come on let's rap for the birds and the bees,

the seals and the fish in the deep blue seas.

The budgies and hamsters sit in their cage,

the lions and tigers roar with rage.

The alligator sees the kangaroo:

»It's a very nice meal.« Would you like it, too?

What is wrong?

What is wrong with Hacky's computer programme? The sentences about the Cool Family are wrong! Can you help him?

Put the sentences right, please.

1. Mr and Mrs Cool – have lunch – never – in the city centre.
2. listens to – the pet radio programme – Mrs Cool – on Friday. – often
3. at work. – plays a computer game – She – sometimes
4. her homework. – Holly Cool – does – never
5. before school. – She – it from her friend – gets – always
6. water – often – Holly and Bolly – on their teacher`s chair. – put
7. with their pets. – go to bed – always – They
8. sleeps – Holly – with her mouse. – always
9. sometimes – in his bed. – teaches his rabbit tricks – Bolly

Can you make three more sentences for a friend?

Dialogues

A ticket, please!

Put in: me – you – it

»I want to go to the zoo.
Can you give ....①.... your bus ticket?«
»Oh, sorry, I can't give ....②.... my ticket.
I haven't got ....③.... here at home.
It's in my hockey bag at school.«

A new programme

Put in: you – us – it

Here are the two rap DJs from Radio York!
You can listen to ....④.... every day.
And when you phone ....⑤.... , we listen to ....⑥.... .
Today we start a new programme.
Listen to ....⑦.... , phone ....⑧.... and say:
»I like ....⑨.... !« or say :
»I think ....⑩.... is boring.«

Pets and animals
practice
answers on page 52
47

The Gossip Game

Für dieses Spiel setzt du dich mit einigen anderen
Mitspielern in einen Kreis. Du flüsterst dem neben dir
Sitzenden einen längeren englischen Satz zu, z.B.

»Susy Softwood often goes to the zoo by bus.«

Dein Nachbar hört zu und gibt den Satz leise weiter, bis der letzte
im Kreis das Gehörte laut ausspricht. Oft kommen dabei lustige Sätze
heraus. Den zweiten Satz flüstert dann dein Nachbar usw.

Dieses Spiel kennt keine Gewinner oder Verlierer, dafür trainiert es aber eine
wichtige Fähigkeit in der Fremdsprache: das genaue Zuhören und Verstehen.

Viel Spaß!

**»Ruby Roftcook
often rolls
to the shoe
by nuts.«**

Lerntipp: *present simple*

Auf den letzten acht Seiten ist dir immer wieder dieselbe Zeitform begegnet, so zum Beispiel:

I like my boyfriend.
Susy often goes to the zoo.
Freddy always walks to the pet shop.
We listen to you.

Diese Zeitform heißt auf Englisch **present simple**, **simple present** oder **simple form**. Die deutsche Übersetzung dafür lautet »einfache Gegenwart«.

Man benutzt sie hauptsächlich, um über Dinge zu sprechen, die regelmäßig passieren, aber auch für solche, die nie oder nur manchmal passieren.

Deswegen kommen in Aussagen im **present simple** sehr oft folgende Wörter vor: **always**, **often**, **every day**, aber auch **sometimes**, **never**.

Merkspruch:
Always, often, every day: dann ist die simple form o.k.!

Natürlich hast du auch gemerkt, dass die **simple form** an einer gewissen Stelle gar nicht so »simpel« ist: Bei **he**, **she** und **it** wird an das Verb nämlich noch ein **-s** angehängt.

Merkspruch:
He, she, it, das »s« geht mit!

Can you do the shnickshnack?

Can you find the shnickshnack words in the sentences?

clean

cat

basket

name

black

My pet is a small shnickshnack.
Her shnickshnack is Pussy.
She is shnickshnack and white.
She sleeps in a brown shnickshnack in my room.
I shnickshnack it every week.

Have you got a cat?
Here is a short rhyme for cats:

> Pussy cat, pussy cat, lank and lean,
> Going to London to look at the Queen.
> Pussy cat, pussy cat, what will you do there?
> I'll frighten a mouse under her chair.

Can you make another rhyme with a pet? It's easy!

My favourite pet

Hast du ein Haustier – oder wünschst du dir eins?
Dann fällt es dir sicher nicht schwer, eine Zeichnung
oder sogar ein Poster davon zu machen.

Mit ein wenig Hilfe kannst du auch auf Englisch etwas
zu deiner Zeichnung schreiben, zum Beispiel:

This is my ...
This is a ... (budgie / dog / cat / hamster / goldfish ...)

His / her colour is ... (white / brown / green / blue / red ...)
His / her name is ...
He / she is big / small ...
He / she eats ...

I can ...
... play with her / him
... teach her / him tricks
... go for a walk with her / him
...

Zeige dein Poster doch einmal deinen Freunden oder –
wenn du dir ein Haustier wünschst – deinen Eltern.
Vielleicht wird dein Wunsch sogar eher erfüllt, als du denkst!

Answers Chapter 4: Pets and animals

p. 42: 1. wild animals 2. pets 3. often, York 4. sometimes, walks
5. lions 6. budgies 7. loves, dolphins 8. rabbits

p. 43: 1. a) meet, b) buy, c) say, d) have
2. a) do, b) look, c) clean, d) get
3. a) think, b) make, c) see, d) give, e) play

p. 44: 1. a) her, b) him, c) her, d) them
2. a) them, b) him, c) them, d) them

p. 46: 1. Mr and Mrs Cool never have lunch in the city centre.
2. Mrs Cool often listens to the pet radio programme on Friday.
3. She sometimes plays a computer game at work.
4. Holly Cool never does her homework.
5. She always gets it from her friend before school.
6. Holly and Bolly often put water on their teacher's chair.
7. They always go to bed with their pets.
8. Holly always sleeps with her mouse.
9. Bolly sometimes teaches his rabbit tricks in his bed.

p. 47: 1. me, 2. you, 3. it, 4. us, 5. us, 6. you, 7. us, 8., us, 9. it, 10. it

p. 50: cat – name – black – basket – clean

Ricky's birthday party

Ricky Riverside's 13th birthday is on 2nd June, and his friends are coming to his birthday party on Saturday.

Ricky gets nice presents: two books about dogs from Emmy, four CDs from Susy and Freddy, a lovely goldfish from Rocky and a very BIG ice-cream birthday cake with thirteen candles from his parents.

They play games and dance to the music of Ricky's new CDs. Then they eat the wonderful cake and drink an awful lot of cola. Later they have sausages with chips, tomato ketchup and cola again. Ups! Of course, they do not feel very well on Sunday, and Emmy has a bad dream at night!

Do you remember?

1. Answer the questions, please.

   a) Is it Ricky's 12th birthday?
   b) Is it on 1st July?
   c) What day is it, a Friday or a Saturday?
   d) Are the books from Emmy?
   e) What is Rocky's present?
   f) What is on the birthday cake?

2. There are two wrong words in each sentence.
Can you find them? Write them on a paper, please.

Example
They play hockey and dance to the video.   **Wrong: hockey / video**

   a) They dance to the music of Susy's old CDs.
   b) They eat the goldfish and drink water.
   c) Later they have fish and chips with lemonade.
   d) They do not feel very bad on Monday.
   e) Rocky has a wonderful dream at night.

A number puzzle

Write the missing number on a paper, please.

Birthdays
puzzle

55

answers on page 64

Example:
Numbers from one to seven:
• **one** • **seven** • **five** • **six** • **two** • **three** • **?** •   **?** = **four**

1. Numbers from one to eight:
   • **three** • **eight** • **seven** • **one** • **six** • **five** • **four** • **?** •

2. Numbers from nine to sixteen:
   • **twelve** • **ten** • **sixteen** • **fourteen** • **nine** • **eleven** • **fifteen** • **?** •

3. Numbers from seventeen to twenty-four:
   • **twenty-three** • **eighteen** • **twenty-two** • **nineteen** • **twenty-one** • **seventeen** • **twenty** • **?** •

4. Numbers from twenty-five to thirty-one:
   • **twenty-six** • **twenty-nine** • **thirty-one** • **twenty-seven** • **twenty-eight** • **twenty-five** • **?** •

Can you make new number puzzles for your friends?

The days of the week

Can you find the days of the week?
Write them on a paper. Start with 1.

1. Our week at school starts with that day.
2. Our week at school ends on that day.
3. Most shops are closed on that day.
4. That day has got the letter »h« in it.
5. You don't go to school on that day, but you can go shopping.
6. It's the second school day of the week.
7. It is a day in the middle of the week.

Now look at your paper and take these
letters from your words:

Take the fifth letter from number 4.
Take the fifth letter from number 2.
Take the second letter from number 3.
Take the first letter from number 5.
Take the fifth letter from number 1.
Take a »g«.
Take the fifth letter from number 7.
Take the fourth letter from number 6.

**The new word is what a lot of kids eat at
birthday parties. Remember Ricky's party!**

The Spelling Relay Game

Mit diesem Spiel kannst du zusammen mit Freunden euer Wortschatzgedächtnis, das richtige Schreiben von englischen Wörtern und das Nachschlagen in Wörterbüchern trainieren, ohne dass Langeweile aufkommt. Ihr benötigt nur Papier und Stifte.

Zunächst einigt ihr euch auf einen Anfangsbuchstaben für das erste Wort. Dann schreibt jeder Mitspieler auf seinem Zettel eine englische Wortreihe auf, bei der jedes folgende Wort immer mit dem Buchstaben beginnt, mit dem das vorhergehende Wort geendet hat.

Beispiel: three – eat – tomato – old – dream – miss – snake ...

Wer zuerst zehn Wörter gefunden hat, ruft: »Stop!«

Die richtig geschriebenen Wörter werden zusammengezählt. Für jedes falsch geschriebene Wort (eventuell im Wörterbuch oder im Englischbuch nachschauen) gibt es einen Punktabzug. Wer die meisten Punkte erreicht, gewinnt.

Where are
a – e – i – o – u – y?

Hier sind nicht nur die Buchstaben durcheinander
geraten, sondern es fehlen auch die Vokale und
das »y« in allen Wörtern. Um welche Wörter handelt
es sich?

1. lJ

2. btrc

3. nJ

4. M

5. tsg

6. plr

7. cDmrb

8. rhMc

9. rrbF

10. brSmtp

11. mvNrb

12. nJr

Hast du noch keine Idee? Dann überlege, ob die Großbuchstaben
oder die Anzahl der Wörter (12!) etwas zu bedeuten haben.
Bringe die Wörter zum Schluss in eine sinnvolle Reihenfolge.

»-s« / »-es« or not?

Can you find the right words?
Write them on a paper, please.

Example:	
teach	The teacher **teaches** the boys and girls, and Mr Hickup often **teaches** his dog.

do   We always ....①.... our job, and you ....②.... your job.

do   Emmy usually ....③.... her homework in her room.

play   Ricky and Rocky sometimes ....④.... in the road.

throw / bring   When I ....⑤.... a stick, my dog never ....⑥.... it back.

ask   Mrs Tictac often ....⑦.... the girls and boys questions at school.

ask   Susy sometimes ....⑧.... Emmy about her homework.

say / help   Then Emmy usually ....⑨.... :
»Okay, Susy, I can ....⑩.... you.«

Lerntipp: Satzstellung

Die Zeitform **present simple** kennst du bereits
(siehe Lerntipp auf S. 49).

Bei dieser Zeitform ordnen sich die Satzteile in ihrer
Reihenfolge zunächst so wie im Deutschen auch:
**Zuerst kommt das Subjekt, dann das Verb, dann das Objekt –
auf Englisch: *subject, verb, object*. Beispiel: Susy likes animals.**

Merkspruch: Im *present* geht es so: S – V – O

Wenn du dich an den Lerntipp auf S. 49 erinnerst oder dir noch einmal die
Übung auf der vorhergehenden Seite ansiehst, wirst du bemerken, dass
im **present simple** ganz bestimmte Wörter, die nicht zu den Satzteilen
subject, verb, object gehören, besonders oft verwendet werden:
Es sind Wörter wie: **always, often, usually, sometimes, never,** ...

Diese Wörter nennt man »Häufigkeitsadverbien« (auf Englisch: *adverbs of
frequency*). Wenn du jetzt die Sätze auf der vorigen Seite genau durchliest,
merkst du auch, an welcher Stelle sie immer stehen:

**Die Häufigkeitsadverbien stehen zwischen dem Subjekt *(subject)*
und dem Verb *(verb)*.** Das muss man sich besonders gut merken,
weil dies anders ist als in unserer Sprache!
Beispiel: Susy geht oft in den Zoo. – **Susy often goes to the zoo.**

A dino race

Can you find the right words?
Write them on a paper.

Example: Number thirteen is the first.

Number five is the ....
Number thirty-one is the ....
Number twenty-two is the ....
Number fifteen is the ....
Number three is the ....
Number thirty is the ....
Number twenty-eight is the ....
Number twelve is the ....

Can you find the sentences?

Put the words in the sentences in the right order.
Look at page 60 for help.

1.
to Mrs Tomorrowlooky. / often / Carla / goes

2.
always / sings / Tina / on Saturdays. / nice songs /

3.
plays football / sometimes / Tim / after school.

4.
Pit / his garden work / at the weekend. / likes / never /

5.
big hamburgers / Tom / often / for lunch. / eats /

6.
Sandra / always / in the evening. / takes Fiffy / for a walk /

7.
never / Mark / makes / good music.

8.
in his room. / plays tennis / Pat /sometimes

Ricky's birthday calendar

→ DONT FORGET!!! BIRTHDAYS:

JANUARY: 3RD: FREDDY	FEBRUARY: 11th: MUM	MARCH: 12TH: SUSY
APRIL: 5TH ROCKY	MAY: 8TH DAD	JUNE: 2ND: ME!!!!
JULY: 1ST: JANE	AUGUST: 9TH GRANDMA	SEPTEMBER: 20TH AUNT MARY
OCTOBER: 31ST MRS TICTAC	NOVEMBER: 22ND: EMMY!!	DECEMBER: 30TH UNCLE JOE

1. Ask a partner: When is Emmy's / Freddy's / Grandma's ... birthday?

2. Write the birthdays on a paper with the numbers in words (the way you speak the dates).

Example: »Freddy's birthday is on the third of January.«

3. Play a game with a partner: Look at the calendar for two minutes. Then close the book and remember the birthdays.

Answers Chapter 5: Birthdays

p. 54: 1. a) No, it's his 13th birthday. b) No, it's on 2nd June. c) It's
         a Saturday. d) Yes, they are. e) It's a goldfish. f) Thirteen candles.
         2. a) Susy's / old, b) goldfish / water, c) fish / lemonade,
         d) bad / Monday, e) Rocky / wonderful

p. 55: 1. two, 2. thirteen, 3. twenty-four, 4. thirty

p. 56: 1. Monday, 2. Friday, 3. Sunday, 4. Thursday, 5. Saturday, 6. Tuesday 7. Wednesday – sausages

p. 58: 1. July, 2. October, 3. June, 4. May, 5. August , 6. April, 7. December, 8. March, 9. February,
         10. September, 11. November, 12. January – January, February, March, April, May, June …

p. 59: 1. do, 2. do, 3. does, 4. play, 5. throw, 6. brings , 7. asks, 8. asks, 9. says, 10. help

p. 61: a) second, b) third, c) fourth, d) fifth, e) sixth, f) seventh, g) eigth, h) ninth

p. 62: 1. Carla often goes to Mrs Tomorrowlooky. 2. Tina always sings nice songs on Saturdays.
         3. Tim sometimes plays football after school. 4. Pit never likes his garden work at the weekend.
         5. Tom often eats big hamburgers for lunch. 6. Sandra always takes Fiffy for a walk in the evening.
         7. Mark never makes good music. 8. Pat sometimes plays tennis in his room.

p. 63: 2. a) Mum's birthday is on the eleventh of February. b) Susy's birthday is on the twelfth of March.
         c) Rocky's birthday is on the fifth of April. d) Dad's birthday is on the eighth of May. e) Ricky's birthday
         is on the second of June. f) Jane's birthday is on the first of July. g) Grandma's birthday is on the
         ninth of August. h) Aunt Mary's birthday is on the twentieth of September. i) Mrs Tictac's birthday is
         on the thirty-first of October. j) Emmy's birthday is on the twenty-second of November. k) Uncle Joe's
         birthday is on the thirtieth of December.

Emmy's dream

The night after Ricky's party
Emmy has a bad dream.
She is standing in a clothes shop with her friend Tina, and she is trying on a lot of new clothes:
– A red pullover, but Tina is laughing: »Terrible!«
– Blue jeans, but Tina is telling her: »Too long!«
– A yellow skirt, but Tina is shouting: »Too short!«
– Black trousers, but Tina is shouting: »Too big!«
– A blue shirt, but Tina is screaming: »Too small!«
– Emmy is getting warmer and warmer. Tina is shouting louder and louder ...
Her mother comes in and wakes her up: »Hey, Emmy, why are you shouting? Are you dreaming?
And let's open the window, it's too warm here.«

Tell the story

You can tell the story again
when you put the sentences together.

1. The night after the party
2. She is standing
3. Tina is
4. She is trying on
5. Tina is telling her the pullover
6. She is shouting: »The skirt
7. She is screaming: »The shirt
8. Emmy is getting
9. Her mother
10. It's too warm

a) is too short!«
b) is terrible.
c) new clothes.
d) warmer and warmer.
e) Emmy has a bad dream.
f) wakes her up.
g) in the shop, too.
h) in a clothes shop.
i) in Emmy's room.
j) is too small!«

Example:
1. e) The night after the party
Emmy has a bad dream.

Micky's Clothes Shop

Find the right words for the pictures and write them on a paper, please.

Example: 1 = m) pullover

a) tah   b) kacjet
c) strithawes   d) eti
e) triks   f) strih
g) sorterus   h) kocss
i) nesja   j) hosse
k) sdres   l) shgitt
m) lupoverl   n) subleo

Lerntipp: Vokabeln lernen mit dem Kassettenrekorder

Hast du den Lerntipp »Vokabeln lernen« auf S. 33 schon gelesen? Wenn nicht, schau ihn dir doch einmal an, ehe du den nächsten Absatz liest.

Eine besonders gute Methode für Kinder, die ihre Vokabeln alleine lernen, ist das Üben mit dem Kassettenrekorder.

Suche dir die Vokabeln heraus (höchstens 12), die du lernen möchtest. Sprich die Wörter auf Deutsch so auf eine Kassette, dass nach jedem Wort eine Pause von ca. 5 Sekunden entsteht; danach sagst du das englische Wort. Ist diese Aufnahme »im Kasten«, stellst du den Rekorder auf *Play* und lässt die Kassette abspielen. In die Pausen hinein sprichst du jeweils das deiner Meinung nach richtige englische Wort und erhältst gleich darauf die Bestätigung, ob deine Lösung richtig war.

Lernst du bereits im zweiten Jahr Englisch? Dann kannst du die Anzahl der Wörter nach einigen Wochen bis auf 20 steigern.

Viel Erfolg!

At the shopping centre

Match the questions and the answers.

1. Why is that boy looking at me?

a) No, I'm looking for the latest techno hit.

b) They are cleaning them.

3. Is that dog barking at us?

5. Are you looking for the new Rocky Randolph CD?

e) Oh yes, that's Benny, let's get out of here.

4. What are the two men doing with the toys?

d) They are looking at a funny comic.

c) Well, because he loves you.

2. Why are the girls laughing?

What are they doing?

a) Find out what the people in the pictures are doing. Write the answers on a paper, please.

Four kids ....❶.... a school uniform.
Three men ....❷.... big boxes.
A boy ....❸.... a CD.
A woman ....❹.... a taxi.
Two ladies ....❺.... shopping.
A girl ....❻.... the assistant a question.
Two boys ....❼.... newspapers.

b) Answer the questions, please. Make short answers.

Example: Are the kids wearing jeans? – No, they aren't.

1. Are the men carrying boxes?
2. Is the boy driving a go-cart?
3. Is the woman driving a taxi?
4. Are the two ladies running?
5. Is the girl answering a question?
6. Are the boys selling newspapers?

The Why-Because-Game

Shopping and clothes
game
71
answers on page 76

Gehörtes und Gelesenes besser verstehen.

Suche zuerst unten die passenden Antworten zu den sieben Fragen heraus und notiere die richtigen Paare. Bastle dann 14 Karten und schreibe auf jede Karte eine Frage oder Antwort. Jetzt werden alle Karten gemischt und in möglichst gleicher Anzahl an die Spielteilnehmer verteilt. Es spielt keine Rolle, ob jemand nur Frage- oder Antwortkarten oder beides bekommt. Die Besitzer von Fragekarten lesen ihre Fragen vor, diejenigen mit der passenden Antwort melden sich und lesen sie vor, bis alle Fragen beantwortet sind. Du kannst dieses Spiel anschließend beliebig um weitere Fragen und Antworten ergänzen.

Hier folgen die 14 Fragen und Antworten:

1. Why is Emmy's mum opening the window? 2. Why can't English kids wear jeans at school? 3. Why aren't Freddy and Mark wearing tights? 4. Why can't you buy newspapers in a clothes shop? 5. Why isn't Susy's baby brother climbing onto the table? 6. Why are you putting on a coat? 7. Why is Emmy buying a Rocky Randolph CD?

a) Because they are boys. b) Because they must wear school uniform. c) Because it's too warm in the room. d) Because it's too cold. e) Because she likes his music. f) Because you can only get clothes there. g) Because it's too high for him.

Telephone calls

Find the missing parts of the dialogues.

Example: »*Let's go shopping in the city.*«
»*No, I can't. I'm cooking a meal.*« | cook a meal

»*Come on, let's go to the Ricky Randolph Concert.*« | write a letter
»*No, I can't.* ❶ ....«

»*Can we go to the cinema, Emmy and Tina?*« | do our homework
»*No, we can't.* ❷ ....«

»*Can Ricky come and help me?*« | sleep
»*No, he can't.* ❸ ....«

»*Can Emmy come and play a computer game with me?*« | go for a walk
»*No, she can't.* ❹ ....«

»*Can Ricky and Rocky play football with me?*« | work in the garden
»*No, they can't.* ❺ ....«

»*Can Freddy come to the phone, please?*« | sit on the toilet
»*No, he can't.* ❻ ....«

Lerntipp: *present progressive*

Hast du dir schon die Lerntipps »*present simple*« und »Satzstellung« angesehen? Wenn nicht, solltest du sie erst einmal auf S. 49 und S. 60 nachschlagen und anschließend im nächsten Absatz weiterlesen.

Während man in der Zeitform **present simple** Dinge ausdrückt, die regelmäßig, manchmal oder nie geschehen, beschreibt man mit dem **present progressive**, das dir auf den letzten acht Seiten immer wieder begegnet ist, **Handlungen oder Situationen, die gerade stattfinden,** wenn man über sie spricht.

Beispiele:
I'm listening to a CD. – Ich höre gerade eine CD.
You are standing on my foot! – Du stehst auf meinem Fuß!
It's raining. – Es regnet gerade.
He is doing his homework. – Er macht jetzt gerade seine Hausarbeiten.

Wie du siehst, bildet man diese Zeit **mit einer Form von** *to be* (siehe Lerntipp »*to be*«, S. 24) **und einem** *-ing* **hinter dem Verb.** Man nennt diese Form daher auch oft »*-ing*-Form«.

Dazu gibt es einen Merkspruch:
Hier und jetzt und guck mal da:
dann kommt die *-ing*-Form, ist doch klar!

Wednesday afternoon in Fulford

Write down the questions and answers.
Use the present progressive.

Example: Mark / music / make?   No / book. / read
Is Mark making music?   **No, he is reading a book.**

1. clean / Mrs Riverside / her car?   No / do / the shopping.

2. eat / a goldfish / Ricky and Rocky?   No / a hamburger. / eat

3. »you / watch TV, Susy?«   »No / a book.« / read

4. buy / a new tie? / Mr Riverside   No / in the garden. / work

5. Tina / try on / new clothes?   No / play / with her baby brother.

In the city

A snake sentence

Can you find the words in these six sentences?
Write them on a paper.

alotofpeoplearewalkingintotheshopsamotherisbuyingicecreamforherchildrenawomaninalongcoatisaskingapolicemanfortheway totheshoppingcentreayoungmaninpinkjeansissellingsweatshirtsinfrontofaclothesshopthreegirlsinschooluniformaretryingonnewhatsamanisputtingnewtrousersandskirtsintoashopwindow

Answers Chapter 6: Shopping and clothes

p. 66:   2. h), 3. g), 4. c), 5. b), 6. a), 7. j), 8. d), 9. f), 10. i)

p. 67:   2 = i) jeans, 3 = k) dress, 4 = b) jacket, 5 = g) trousers,
6 = c) sweatshirt, 7 = a) hat, 8 = f) shirt, 9 = e) skirt, 10 = d) tie,
11 = h) socks, 12 = l) tights, 13 = n) blouse, 14 = j) shoes

p. 69:   1. c), 2. d), 3. e), 4. b), 5. a)

p. 70:   a) 1. are wearing, 2. are carrying, 3. is buying, 4. is driving. 5. are going, 6. is asking, 7. are selling
b) 1. Yes, they are. 2. No, he isn't. 3. Yes, she is. 4. No, they aren't. 5. No, she isn't. 6. Yes, they are.

p. 71:   1. c), 2. b), 3. a), 4. f), 5. g), 6. d), 7. e)

p. 72:   1. I'm writing a letter. 2. We are doing our homework. 3. He is sleeping, 4. She is going for a walk.
5. They are working in the garden. 6. He is sitting on the toilet.

p. 74:   1. Is Mrs Riverside cleaning her car? – No she is doing the shopping.
2. Are Ricky and Rocky eating a goldfish? – No, they are eating a hamburger.
3. »Are you watching TV, Susy?« – »No, I'm reading a book.«
4. Is Mr Riverside buying a new tie? – No, he is working in the garden.
5. Is Tina trying on new clothes? – No, she is playing with her baby brother.

p. 75:   A lot of people are walking into the shops. A mother is buying ice cream for her children.
A woman in a long coat is asking a policeman for the way to the shopping centre. A young man
in pink jeans is selling sweatshirts in front of a clothes shop. Three girls in school uniform are
trying on new hats. A man is putting new trousers and skirts into a shop window.

Tina's week at school

Tina Tornado goes to school in Kingston. Her favourite subject is Music: the Music teacher looks like a pop star! She likes Art and P.E., too, because there is no homework. Science (that's Physics, Biology, Chemistry) and Technology are o.k., but History and French are boring. Tina really hates only one subject: Maths. The teacher is so old, he looks like an elephant and he always gives a lot of homework!

Timetable for: Tina Tornado

Monday	Tuesday	Wednesday	Thursday	Friday
Maths	English	Science	P.E.*	English
English	Maths	R.E.*	English	Geography
P.E.*	Technology	History	Maths	Science
L U N C H				
Geography	French	Music	Science	English
Art	Drama*	French	Technology	-----------

* P.E. = Physical Education (sports)
R.E. = Religious Education
Drama = Acting scenes, theatre club, role plays

Do you get everything right?

Remember Tina's school week and find out
what is right: a), b), or c)

1. Tina's favorite subject is
   a) Music.
   b) Pop Music.
   c) P.E.

2. The Music teacher looks like a
   a) tennis star.
   b) football star.
   c) pop star.

3. Tina likes
   a) Art and Science.
   b) P.E. and Technology.
   c) Art and P.E.

4. These subjects are o.k. for Tina
   a) Science and Technology.
   b) History and Technology.
   c) French and Science.

5. These subjects are boring
   a) Maths and History.
   b) French and German.
   c) French and History.

6. The Maths teacher is
   a) cold.
   b) old.
   c) owl.

7. He looks like an
   a) e-mail.
   b) elk.
   c) elephant.

8. He gives a
   a) dot of Homework.
   b) lot of homework.
   c) bit of homework.

A subject scramble

Find out the subjects and write them down, please.

Example: 1.= **ENGLISH**

1. NEGSHIL
2. GOLIBOY
3. MARAD
4. TAR
5. CNEHRF
6. SCHISPY
7. THYROSI
8. MERGAN
9. PHYRAGGOE
10. LOCHNETGOY
11. NECCIES
12. SCHMIERTY
13. HAMST
14. SUCIM
15. GORISULIE TADENOICU
16. SCHALPYI NOTICADEU

Stella Strict

Stella Strict works in the school cafeteria at Tina's school in Kingston. She has got a hard job with the kids. She has to tell them a lot of things!

Write the missing words on a paper, please.
Put in »must« or »must not«.

1. You ...**1**... put your shoes on the tables!
2. You ...**2**... smoke here!
3. You ...**3**... take away the bottles from the table!
4. You ...**4**... leave your places clean!
5. You ...**5**... stay here after the end of breaks!
6. You ...**6**... close the doors to the toilets!
7. You ...**7**... turn your music too loud!
8. You ...**8**... pay for your cola before you leave!

School puzzle

What is there at school or what can you see in a school building?

Find the 14 words in the puzzle and write them on a paper, please.

You can find words across, down and diagonally!*

Example:
1. TABLE

A	B	C	T	A	B	L	E	D	C	E
V	O	S	C	H	M	W	C	Q	H	P
X	W	G	M	B	C	P	P	Z	A	B
E	V	I	O	P	X	L	H	X	I	D
D	U	R	N	E	P	Q	X	Y	R	P
O	R	L	V	D	B	B	T	H	B	I
O	E	W	X	Y	O	I	O	V	Q	C
R	P	C	N	M	A	W	S	Y	A	T
A	O	L	E	N	R	B	P	L	O	U
B	V	P	D	R	D	X	E	T	M	R
F	L	O	O	R	K	L	N	M	W	E
X	Z	S	T	U	E	B	C	O	A	Z
S	A	T	L	L	K	X	I	Z	C	H
B	I	E	O	E	D	Q	L	P	M	N
H	G	R	U	R	M	W	A	L	L	X

*Die Lösungswörter findest du waagerecht (drei Wörter), senkrecht (acht Wörter) und diagonal (drei Wörter).

Die diagonalen Lösungswörter werden alle von links oben nach rechts unten gelesen.

Ten rules for the Funny Little Dino School

Here are the ten rules for a school for little dinos.

1. You must be late for school.
2. You should not say »Good morning« to the teachers.
3. Teachers should give you a glass of cola or lemonade every day.
4. You should eat and drink in the classroom.
5. You must not listen to the teachers.
6. You don't have to read at school.
7. You should listen to pop music in the classroom.
8. You must not clean the board after a lesson.
9. You don't have to do your homework.
10. You must not write tests.

Look at the rules. They are funny, but they are very different from the rules at our school.

Can you correct the rules?
Write the correct rules on a paper.

The Chain Game

Das *chain game* oder Kettenspiel ist dir
in ähnlicher Form sicher bereits begegnet.

In diesem Spiel kommt es darauf an, einen begonnenen
Satz pro Spieler immer wieder durch ein neues Wort zu
ergänzen, bis der Satz so lang geworden ist, dass einer der
Mitspieler einen Fehler beim Wiederholen des bisherigen Satzes macht.

Du kannst zusammen mit deinen Freunden bei diesem Spiel nicht nur
das Gedächtnis, sondern auch noch deinen Vokabelschatz und die
richtige Anwendung der Vokabeln trainieren.

> Der erste Mitspieler beginnt z.B. mit: **»On ...«**, der zweite macht
> weiter mit: **»On Monday ...«**, der dritte mit: **»On Monday, I ...«**, der
> vierte sagt: **»On Monday, I always ...«**, der fünfte: **»On Monday,
> I always go ...«** usw.

Wenn ihr zwei Gruppen von Spielern bilden könnt, kann man das
chain game natürlich auch als Wettspiel nutzen.

> Nützliche Verben zum Einsatz in diesem Spiel sind:
> **read – run – do – wear – go – play – write – help – clean – listen –
> watch – make – wash – talk – work**

School in Britain

In Britain children go to Primary School when they are 5 years old. Most of them change to Comprehensive School when they are 11. They leave school when they are 16 or older. A lot of kids must wear school uniform. Do you like it?

School is from nine o'clock in the morning to four o'clock in the afternoon. After that there is still homework to do! A long school day, isn't it?

The pupils can have lunch at a school cafeteria. There are no classrooms at Comprehensive Schools. The kids have to walk to another room at the end of a lesson.

Lerntipp: modale Hilfsverben

Was sind eigentlich modale Hilfsverben?
Ganz einfach, dahinter verbergen sich solche Wörter
wie **can, can't, must, must not, have to, don't have to,
should, should not.**

Sie sind dir auf den vorherigen Seiten immer wieder begegnet.
Während die ersten beiden *(can – can't)* uns fast keine Schwierigkeiten
bereiten, weil sie ähnlich wie im Deutschen klingen und auch so verwendet
werden, kann man sich an die anderen nur schwer gewöhnen. Deshalb sind hier
die wichtigsten modalen Hilfsverben noch einmal zusammengefasst:

must	**etwas müssen**
must not	**etwas nicht dürfen** (Verbot)
should	**etwas lieber tun sollen** (Empfehlung)
should not	**etwas lieber nicht tun sollen** (Empfehlung)
have to	**etwas müssen**
don't have to	**etwas nicht müssen**

Natürlich fällt dir auf, dass **must** und **have to** beide »müssen« bedeuten. In der
Gegenwartsform kannst du daher beides benutzen. Du kannst jedoch **must**
nicht in die Vergangenheit setzen, wohl aber **have to** (wird zu **had to**).
Noch etwas ist schwierig zu merken: bei **must / must not**, **should / should not**
und auch bei **can / can't** gibt es kein **-s** bei **he / she / it**, wohl aber bei **have to**
(**has to**) und **don't have to** (**doesn't have to**).

Hier hilft wirklich nur eins: Man muss diese Wörter lernen wie Vokabeln.

A Sunday with the Rowdy Family

The Rowdies have got four children.
They ask a lot of questions on Sundays.

Put in: must – must not – should – should not – don't have to
The first letters of the missing words are already there.
Write the words on a paper, please.

Remmy: M......① I wear uniform today?

Mrs R.: No, you d......② wear it today.

Demmy: M......③ I have a shower today?

Mr R.: Yes, you m......④ have a shower.

Mrs R.: Hey, Remmy! You m......⑤ play with the sandwich!

Rinky: M......⑥ I clean the car today?

Mr R.: No, you d......⑦ clean it today.

Mrs R.: Dinky, you m......⑧ clean your bike in the house!

Remmy: Mum is working. M......⑨ she always work?

Mr R.: No, you s......⑩ help her, children!

Dinky: Dad, you s......⑪ read a book now. We s......⑫ all help her.

Englisch lernen im Internet

Zum Thema Englisch lernen gibt es eine Fülle von Adressen im weltweiten Netz, aber nur wenige sind für Englischlerner in den ersten beiden Lehrjahren wirklich nützlich. Deshalb sind hier einige Adressen aufgeführt, die wir für dich überprüft haben.

Wenn Fragen in Englisch auftauchen, deren Antworten dir Schwierigkeiten machen, kannst du dich an eine Hotbox wenden.

Unter **www.hausaufgaben.de** drückst du auf die Schaltfläche »Willkommen bei www.hausaufgaben.de«, anschließend klickst du den Begriff »Hotbox« und dann »Hotbox Englisch« an. Es erscheint ein Feld, in das du deine Frage eingeben und gleich darauf abschicken kannst. Sie wird recht rasch beantwortet. Ein gut funktionierendes und einfach zu bedienendes Online-Wörterbuch Deutsch-Englisch und Englisch-Deutsch kannst du unter **www.tu-chemnitz.de/urz/netz/forms/dict.html** abrufen.

Für diejenigen von euch, die bereits unregelmäßige Verben lernen müssen, gibt es unter **www.members.aol.com** ein Trainingsprogramm zum Üben der unregelmäßigen Verben. Wenn du die Adresse eingegeben hast, erscheint eine englischsprachige Seite. Gib nun zusätzlich zur Adresse ein: /**wwwschule**. Auf der nächsten Seite klickst du die Schaltfläche »Vokabeltrainer« an.

Suchst du nach Texten von aktuellen oder älteren Hits oder Songs? Dann ist **www./lyrics-world.de** eine gute Adresse.

Answers Chapter 7: School

p. 78: 1. a), 2. c), 3. c), 4. a), 5. c), 6. b), 7. c), 8 b)

p. 79: 2. Biology, 3. Drama, 4. Art, 5. French, 6. Physics, 7. History,
8. German, 9. Geography, 10. Technology, 11. Science, 12. Chemistry,
13. Maths, 14. Music, 15. Religious Education, 16. Physical Education

p. 80: 1. must not, 2. must not, 3. must, 4. must,
5. must not, 6. must, 7. must not, 8. must

p. 81: ➔

p. 82:
1. You must not be late for school.
2. You should say »Good morning« to the teachers.
3. Teachers should not / must not give
   you a glass of cola or lemonade every day.
4. You must not eat and drink in the classrooms.
5. You should / must listen to the teachers.
6. You must / have to read at school.
7. You must not listen to pop music in the classroom.
8. You must / should clean the board after a lesson.
9. You must / should / have to do your homework.
10. You must write tests.

p. 86: 1. Must, 2. don't have to, 3. Must, 4. must,
5. must not, 6. Must, 7. don't have to, 8. must not,
9. Must, 10. should, 11. should not, 12. should

Free time
for the kids

School is over on Friday.
Tina and the Rowdy kids are talking
about their weekends.

Remmy: Do you go on car trips at the weekends, Tina?

Tina: No, we don't. We often go to a lake by bike, because I like swimming and my parents' hobby is fishing. What do you do?

Demmy: We sometimes go to Scotland by car, because Mum and Dad like the mountains and Remmy and I love sleeping in a tent. But Remmy doesn't enjoy the car trip.

Remmy: I really don't like it. I can't listen to my cassettes, because Little Rinky always jumps around on me when I want to listen to them.

Rinky: Hey! I don't jump on you, I dance to your pop music.

Tina: Aha, holiday time – activity time, don't you know that, Remmy?

Remmy: O.K., but I'm not Little Rinky's personal disco!

Do you remember?

Can you complete the sentences?
Write them on a paper, please.

Be careful, it is not so easy!

Do
Does

like car trips?
go to Scotland by car?
love sleeping in a tent?
jump around on Remmy?
go to a lake by car?
like swimming?

1 ..... the Tornados **2** ..... ?   No, they don't.

3 ..... Tina **4** ..... ?   Yes, she does.

5 ..... the Rowdies **6** ..... ?   Yes, they do.

7 ..... Remmy **8** ..... ?   No, he doesn't.

9 ..... Little Rinky **10** ..... ?   Yes, he does.

11 ..... Remmy and Demmy **12** ..... ?   Yes, they do.

Hobbies and places

I. What goes together? Complete the line, please.

Some places go with more than one hobby, and some hobbies go with more than one place.

Football and playing field, fishing and ...

Hobbies	Places
football	lake
fishing	swimming pool
swimming	the sea
tennis	mountains
computer games	disco
reading	playing field
dancing	a kid's room
music	garden
hiking	park
camping	camping site
riding a horse	river
table tennis	tent
hockey	living room
basketball	school

II. One out of four is wrong in the line. Find the odd one out, please.

Example:
dancing – table tennis – fishing – tests
Wrong: tests

1. Hobbies

a) camping – crying – hiking – fishing
b) tennis – table tennis – office – music
c) fireball – football – basketball – hockey
d) swimming – riding – reading – really

2. Places

a) school – room – rule – living room
b) river – weekend – lake – sea
c) Sunday – tent – camping site – park
d) mountains – moments – disco – garden

Michael Clexxon and Dinoboy

Michael Clexxon is a reporter from »Saurian News«. He is interviewing Dinoboy.

Can you find the answers to the questions?

1. Do you go by car?
2. Do you and your friends go on a trip at the weekend?
3. Do you listen to music on the train, Dinoboy?
4. Do you like rap music?
5. Do your friends like it?
6. Do you have picnics at Fantasy Dino Park?
7. Do your friends have milk with the dinoburger?

a) Yes, I do. Rap is my favourite music.
b) Yes, they do. They often watch cool rap videos together.
c) No, they don't. They always have Red Dino Cola with the macs.
d) No, we don't. We go by dino train.
e) Yes, we do. We often go to Fantasy Dino Park.
f) No, I don't. I sing saurian raps.
g) Yes, we do. We eat big dinomacs.

The Word Quiz Game

Mit diesem Spiel kannst du zusammen mit anderen Mitspielern deine mündliche Sprachgewandtheit besonders gut trainieren.

Ihr braucht dazu nur zwei Teams, die jeweils aus zwei oder mehr Mitspielern bestehen, und einen Spielleiter.

Zuerst werden beide Teams nach draußen geschickt und der Spielleiter schreibt zehn englische Wörter auf einen Zettel. Am besten eignen sich gegenständliche Begriffe. Das erste Team kommt wieder herein, ein Mitglied dieser Mannschaft erhält den Zettel und muss nun in zwei Minuten ein Wort nach dem anderen so erklären, dass sein Team es errät. Das Wort selbst darf er dabei nicht benutzen.

Anschließend wird das zweite Team hereingerufen. Wer in zwei Minuten die meisten Begriffe gefunden hat, gewinnt.

In der nächsten Runde erklärt in jedem Team ein anderer Mitspieler die Begriffe.

Do they like it – or not?

Make questions and answers with »Does ... like ...?«

 = »Yes, he / she does.« = »No, he / she doesn't.«

Example: ... windy holidays at the seeside?
Does Sporty like windy holidays at the seaside? No, he doesn't.

SPORTY
1. ... bike trips?

2. ... holidays in a hotel?

PORKY
3. ... holidays in his tent?

PEGGY TOPCORN
4. ... Tony Ticket?

5. ... hamsters?

BILLY BETTERBODY
6. ... dancing?

7. ... swimming?

SAMMY SLEEPER
8. ... holidays at the sea?

9. ... garden work?

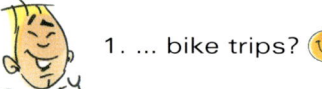
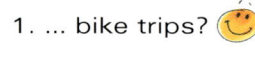

Lerntipp:
Fragen mit *do* und *does*

Wenn du auf Englisch eine Frage stellst, in der Hilfsverben (z.B. Formen von *can / be / have*) stehen, kannst du die Frage wie im Deutschen bilden.

Beispiele: Can you play hockey?
Is Susy reading a comic?
Have the Rowdies got three children?

Wenn aber kein Hilfsverb in der Frage vorkommt, musst du stattdessen do oder (bei he / she / it) does in den Fragesatz einsetzen.

Beispiele: Do you like rap music?
Does she like picnics?
Do they play hockey?
Where do they play hockey?
What does Susy like?
When do they watch TV?

Also: Fragen geh'n mit does und do, das weiß sogar mein linker Schuh!
Und: Sagst du does bei he / she / it, bist du für die Fragen fit!

Tony Ticket's week

Can you find the questions about Tony's week?
Write them on a paper, please.

Free time
practice
answers on page 100

96

1. Where ....①....? He lives in Grimsby.
2. When ....②....? He gets up at half past seven.
3. How ....③....? He gets to school on his bike.
4. What ....④....? At five o'clock in the afternoon he does his homework.
5. What ....⑤....? On Sunday he goes to church.
6. Where ....⑥....? He plays football in the garden.
7. What ....⑦....? On Tuesday he goes swimming.
8. Why ....⑧....? He likes Thursday because he can play in his music group.
9. When ....⑨....? He meets his girlfriend Peggy on Friday.
10. Where ....⑩....? On Saturday he goes to the
    disco with Peggy.

Babsie Bookworm

Babsie Bookworm is Penny's new friend. Penny asks her a lot of questions.

1. Use: Does – Do – Where – When – How – What
Write the missing words on a paper, please.

Penny:

1 ..... do you get up, Babsie?
2 ..... do you have breakfast?
3 ..... do you go to school?
4 ..... your friends have lunch
   together with you?
5 ..... your mother help you
   with your homework?
6 ..... do you do after that?
7 ..... you and your sister
   watch TV together?
8 ..... you go to bed early?

Babsie:

At half past seven.
At home, of course.
I run, because I'm often late.

No, they don't have lunch with me.

No, she doesn't help me.

I usually read books. That's fun for me.

No, we don't. My sister doesn't like it.
No, I don't go to bed early. I read
a lot in the evening.

PENNY

BABSIE
BOOKWORM

2. Look at the answer for 1 minute. Put a paper over
the answer. A partner asks the questions, you answer them.

Lerntipp: Kurzantworten und Verneinungen mit *do* und *does*

Die Kurzantworten mit Hilfsverben kennst du bereits.

Beispiele: Yes, we have. / No, we haven't.

Yes, I am. / No, I'm not.   Yes, he is. / No, he isn't.

Yes, he can. / No, he can't.

Genauso machst du es, wenn du eine Kurzantwort auf eine Frage mit **do** oder **does** (siehe Lerntipp S.95) geben möchtest.

Beispiele: Do you read comics? – Yes, I do. / No, I don't.

Does she like picnics? – Yes, she does. / No, she doesn't.

Do they play basketball? – Yes, they do. / No, they don't.

Jetzt ist es nur noch ein kleiner Schritt, um längere Aussagen mit Verneinungen zu machen. Du brauchst eine verneinte Kurzantwort nämlich nur zu verlängern, um einen verneinten Satz zu bilden.

Beispiele: No, I don't read comics.   No, she doesn't like picnics.

No, they don't play basketball.

Ein Lernspiel basteln

Wie wärs mal mit einem selbst gebastelten Lernspiel?

Du bastelst für jeden Buchstaben des Alphabets eine etwa 10 cm hohe und 5 cm breite Buchstabenkarte aus festem Papier oder Karton. Du kannst auch zuerst die Buchstaben auf Papier malen und sie anschließend auf Karton kleben. Von jedem Buchstaben fertigst du eine Karte an und fertig ist dein Lernspiel!

Mit deinen Mitspielern vereinbarst du jetzt nur noch die Spielregeln. Ihr könnt euch zum Beispiel darauf einigen, nur Verben mit dem Anfangsbuchstaben zu suchen, der auf einer vom Spielleiter hochgehaltenen Buchstabenkarte steht. Wer als Erster ein Verb mit diesem Buchstaben ruft, erhält die Karte. Wer am Schluss die meisten Karten besitzt, ist der Gewinner.

Andere Möglichkeiten sind:

- **Nur Nomen (Substantive) sind gesucht.**
- **Alle Wortarten sind erlaubt.**
- **Der Buchstabe auf der Wortkarte muss der Endbuchstabe sein.**

p. 90: 1. Do, 2. go to a lake by car, 3. Does, 4. like swimming, 5. Do, 6. go to Scotland by car, 7. Does, 8. like car trips, 9. Does, 10. jump around on Remmy, 11. Do, 12. love sleeping in a tent

p. 91: I. ..., fishing and lake/the sea/river, swimming and lake/the sea/river/ swimming pool, tennis and playing field, computer games and a kid's room/school, reading and a kid's room/living room/school, dancing and disco/school, music and a kid's room/living room/school/disco, hiking and mountains, camping and tent/camping site, riding a horse and park/mountains, table tennis and school/garden/camping site, hockey and playing field/school, basketball and playing field/school
II. 1. a) crying, b) office, c) fireball, d) really – 2. a) rule, b) weekend, c) Sunday, d) moments

p. 92: 1.e), 2.d), 3.f), 4.a), 5.b), 6.g), 7.c)

p. 94: 1. Does Sporty like bike trips? Yes, he does. 2. Does Porky like holidays in a hotel? No he doesn't. 3. Does he like holidays in his tent? Yes, he does. 4. Does Peggy Popcorn like Tony Ticket? Yes, she does. 5. Does she like hamsters? No, she doesn't. 6. Does Billy Betterbody like dancing? No, he doesn't. 7. Does he like swimming? Yes, he does. 8. Does Sammy Sleeper like holidays at the sea? Yes, he does. 9. Does he like garden work? No, he doesn't.

p. 96: 1. Where does he live? 2. When does he get up? 3. How does he get to school? 4. What does he do at five o'clock in the afternoon? 5. What does he do on Sunday? 6. Where does he play football? 7. What does he do on Tuesday? 8. Why does he like Thursday? 9. When does he meet his girlfriend Peggy? 10. Where does he go on Saturday?

p. 97: 1. When, 2. Where, 3. How, 4. Do, 5. Does, 6. What, 7. Do, 8. Do

A picnic in Scotland

Last summer Tony Ticket and his parents went to Scotland for their holidays. One day they wanted to have a picnic in the hills. Mrs Ticket bought sausages, eggs and orange juice and she made some sandwiches as well.

Then they had their picnic near a lake. Suddenly Tony saw a lot of men with long red hair and dirty old clothing running and shouting. They really looked frightening! Tony was afraid and ran away as fast as he could. But Mrs Ticket started to laugh.

»Hey, come back, Tony. They're making a film, look at the men with the cameras,« she told him. »Perhaps it's a film about the old Celtic people of Scotland.«

Looking for the questions

Here are the answers to some questions about the picnic in Scotland. Can you find the questions? Write them on a paper, please.

Answers:

1. ❓ To Scotland
2. ❓ No, they didn't.
3. ❓ Sausages, eggs and orange juice.
4. ❓ Yes, she did
5. ❓ Near a lake.
6. ❓ Because he was afraid.
7. ❓ Mrs Ticket started to laugh.
8. ❓ »They're making a film.«

Questions:

make / some sandwiches? / she / Did
to laugh? / started / Who
the Tickets / Where / for their holidays? / go / did
What / Tony? / did / tell / Mrs Ticket
buy? / did / Mrs Ticket / What
Did / they / want to have / in a restaurant / a meal / one day?
Tony / Why / run / away? / did
the picnic? / Where / did / have / they

A food and drink shake

Made by Shakey

Hi, I'm Shakey. I take words and shake them, so they break in two pieces. Can you put the pieces together again? All the words are food and drink words. You can find 14 things to eat and drink.

Examples:
apple pie, milk shake

omelegg

apple shake

cornburger

saladette

meat juice

fishflakes

chickentables

milk pie

letthurt

teresli

orange pie

mubut

vegesoup

yoguce

Tony's holiday letter

Tony Ticket wrote this letter to his girlfriend Peggy Popcorn, but he forgot the **past forms of »be«** in every sentence. Can you find them? Write them on a paper, please.

Hi Peggy,

Here's some news from Scotland:

There ...①... an open bus in Edinburgh, and there ...②... nice beaches near the city. There ...③... a lot of boring girls, but there ...④... no bad day at the seaside. In Scotland there ...⑤... only one windy day, but there ...⑥... no toilets in the mountains. Terrible! There ...⑦... no playground in Gretna Green, but there ...⑧... a nice park behind our hotel. There ...⑨... two girls from London in the park, but there ...⑩... no disco in Gretna Green.

So don't worry about me!
Bye for now
      Love

    Tony

Another detective game

In diesem Spiel geht es wie im ersten Detektivspiel
auf S. 38 darum, herauszufinden, in welche Rolle
ein Mitspieler geschlüpft ist. Dies kann ein Freund
oder eine Freundin, ein Bekannter, Verwandter oder eine
berühmte Persönlichkeit sein. Um es herauszufinden, dürfen
ihm jetzt aber nur Fragen mit *do / does* und *did* gestellt werden,
und zwar so, dass die Antworten jeweils nur mit *yes* oder *no*
beginnen können.

Wenn die Person nach 12 Fragen nicht herausgefunden wurde, hat der
Mitspieler eine Runde gewonnen. Ihr könnt euch auch darauf einigen,
dass vor der ersten Frage eine Angabe zu der zu erratenden Person
gemacht werden muss, z.B. *she / he is a girl / boy /
woman / man / famous person* …

Beispiele für Fragen:

Do you / Does he / she live in …?
.... work at …?
.... play …?
.... like …?
Did you / he / she .... see / her / him yesterday /
last week / last year?

What Sniffy, Becky and Robby did last weekend

Find the right words for each sentence and put them into the past form.

A. feel – look – be – not phone

> **Example: Sniffy was at home.**

He **1** ...... out of the window.
He **2** ...... terrible because his girlfriend **3** ...... him.

B. be – listen – go – tell
Becky **1** ...... to Mrs Taboo.
She **2** ...... to her for half an hour.
Mrs Taboo **3** ...... Becky all about her future.
Becky **4** ...... not very happy after that.

C. cut – work – not like – make
Robby Racket **1** ...... in the garden.
He **2** ...... the grass in the morning.
But he **3** ...... it too much,
because his mower **4** ...... a lot of noise.

Lerntipp: *past simple*

Wie man sich ausdrückt, wenn man etwas aus der Gegenwart erzählen oder schreiben will, hast du in den Lerntipps auf S. 49 und S. 60 gelesen.

Wenn du etwas ausdrücken möchtest, das in der Vergangenheit liegt, also vorbei ist, bringst du die Verben in eine andere Form, die Vergangenheitsform oder *past form*. Das ist im Deutschen genauso wie im Englischen. In der englischen Sprache wird es uns aber wesentlich leichter gemacht: Du hängst an das Verb einfach ein *-ed* an! Das *-s* bei *he / she / it* entfällt sogar auch noch!

Beispiele: *Gegenwart* (present simple)	*Vergangenheit* (past simple)
I watch TV.	I watched TV.
She likes swimming.	She liked swimming.

Eine **Schwierigkeit** gibt es aber doch noch: Bei einigen Verben funktioniert das Anhängen von *-ed* nicht; sie haben eine andere Vergangenheitsform. Man nennt diese Verben daher auch **unregelmäßige** Verben.

Beispiele: Gegenwartsform	Vergangenheitsform
go	went
have/has	had
do	did
am/is; are (von »be«)	was; were
see	saw

Die Vergangenheitsformen dieser unregelmäßigen Verben muss man leider wie Vokabeln einzeln lernen.

The storm

**Find the right words in the sentences.
Write them on a paper, please.**

One Sunday in the holidays Tony and his father
went / looked / listened to a fishing lake.
But there was / wasn't / were a lot of wind and there were no fish.
So in the afternoon they started / visited / ended their trip home.
There were / was no traffic on the road. They didn't / don't / doesn't
know why, but then they saw / heard / watched a weather warning
on the radio. There were / was a terrible storm in Scotland.

Tony feels / felt / finds nervous. Then the storm came / come / comes.
It makes / made / mailed a terrible noise. It washed / walked / wanted
to blow them away. It shot / get / got stronger and stronger.

Then they saw / heard / listened a railway bridge. Mr Ticket cleaned /
stopped / washed the car under it. Now they was / wasn't / were safe.
That was close!

Where are a – e – i – o – u – y?

The letters a – e – i – o – u – y are missing
in the words. Can you find the words?
Write them on a paper, please.

A. Food and drink

1.	orng jc	fshbrgr	ssg	mt
2.	sld	tmt	chs	brd
3.	bttr	sp	chckn	ppl

B. Holiday words

1.	mntn	hll	s	bch
2.	swm	tnt	cmpng	hld
3.	pcnc	lk	htl	trp

Lerntipp: Fragen und Verneinungen im *past simple*

Wie die Vergangenheitsform gebildet wird, hast du schon im Lerntipp auf S. 107 gelesen.

Willst du Fragen oder Verneinungen in der Vergangenheitsform gebrauchen, kannst du in allen Fragen, in denen **do / does** verwendet wird, diese Wörter einfach durch das Wort **did** ersetzen; **don't** und **doesn't** wird zu **didn't**.

Beispiele:	Gegenwart *(present simple)*	Vergangenheit *(past simple)*
	Do you eat lettuce?	Did you eat lettuce?
	I don't eat lettuce.	I didn't eat lettuce.
	Does he drink milk?	Did he drink milk?
	No, he doesn't drink milk.	No, he didn't drink milk.

Fragen und Verneinungen, die ohne **do / does** gebildet werden, weil sie bereits ein Hilfsverb im Satz enthalten, werden einfach in die Vergangenheit gesetzt wie alle anderen Sätze auch.

Beispiele:	Gegenwart *(present simple)*	Vergangenheit *(past simple)*
	I can't open the door.	I couldn't open the door.
	She is not at home.	She was not at home.
	We are in Scotland.	We were in Scotland.

A holiday week

The sentences are all wrong.
Make them right, please.

Example:
They watched a video of Superman on Monday.
No, they **didn't watch** a video of Superman.
They **watched** a video of the old Celtic people of Scotland.

A big dog walked into the Tickets'
hotel room on Tuesday.
No, it ....①.... into the hotel room on
Tuesday. It ....②.... into the hotel room
on Monday.

Mrs Ticket was angry
when she saw the dog.
No, she ....③.... angry.
She ....④.... friendly to the dog.

Tony wrote a letter to Peggy
on Thursday.
No, he ....⑤.... the letter on Thursday.
He ....⑥.... it on Wednesday.

Mr Ticket played tennis on Thursday.
No, he ....⑦.... it on Thursday.
He ....⑧.... it on Friday.

Tony and his new friend Pit were
in the mountains on Saturday.
No, they ....⑨.... in the mountains
on Saturday.
They ....⑩.... there
on Sunday.

A spelling game

Holidays
info
112
answers on page 114

Mit diesem Spiel kannst du zusammen mit Freundinnen oder Freunden das alphabetische Ordnen von Wörtern und den Umgang mit einem Wörterbuch trainieren.

Jeder Spielteilnehmer notiert zunächst eine vereinbarte Zahl von Wörtern – es sollten mindestens 8 bis 12 sein – mit demselben Anfangsbuchstaben. Dann werden alle Zettel so unter den Spielern vertauscht, dass jeder einen anderen Zettel erhält. Jeder versucht nun, die Wörter durch Nummerieren in die richtige alphabetische Reihenfolge zu bringen.

Bei unterschiedlichen Meinungen kann ein Wörterbuch als Schiedsrichter eingesetzt werden, auch dann, wenn man meint, dass ein Wort auf einem Zettel falsch geschrieben wurde.

Komplizierter wird es, wenn ihr euch darauf einigt, dass die **ersten und zweiten** Buchstaben der Wörter gleich sein müssen. In diesem Fall braucht ihr auf jeden Fall ein Wörterbuch, um genügend passende Wörter zu finden.

HOLY 1

HOME 2

HONEY 3

HOOK 4

HORSE 5

HOUSE 6

Holidays in Britain

Here are some of the most famous British areas for nice holidays:

In the **Lake District** you can swim, ride, hike. There are a lot of camping sites.

A lot of people like to take their holidays in **Wales.** They stay in old villages and can go for long walks in the hills.

In **Scotland** you can climb high mountains. Visit Gretna Green. There you can marry when you are 16 years old!

Millions of tourists from all over the world visit **London** every year.

Brighton is a popular place for summer holidays at the seaside.

Do you want more information? Write to: British Tourist Authority, 60325 Frankfurt/M.

Answers Chapter 9: Holidays

p. 102: 1. Where did the Tickets go for their holidays?
2. Did they want to have a meal in a restaurant one day?
3. What did Mrs Ticket buy?
4. Did she make some sandwiches?
5. Where did they have the picnic?
6. Why did Tony run away?
7. Who startet to laugh?
8. What did Mrs Ticket tell Tony?

p. 103: apple pie, yoghurt, milk shake, omelette, fishburger, egg salad, cornflakes, vegetables, lettuce, chicken soup, muesli, orange juice, butter, meat

p. 104: 1. was, 2. were, 3. were, 4. was, 5. was, 6. was, 7. was, 8. was, 9. were, 10. was

p. 106: A. 1. looked, 2. felt, 3. did not phone
B. 1. went, 2. listened, 3. told, 4. was
C. 1. worked, 2. cut, 3. did not like, 4. made

p. 108: went – was – started – was – didn't – heard – was – felt – came – made – wanted – got – saw – stopped – were

p. 109: A. 1. orange juice – fishburger – sausages – meat
2. salad – tomato – cheese – bread 3. butter – soup – chicken – apple
B. 1. mountain – hill – sea – beach 2. swim – tent – camping – holiday
3. picnic – lake – hotel – trip

p. 111: 1. didn't walk, 2. walked, 3. wasn't, 4. was, 5. didn't write, 6. wrote, 7. didn't play, 8. played, 9. weren't, 10. were

Übersicht über die grammatischen Inhalte

Inhalt	Kapitel

- **personal pronouns** (Personalpronomen; I, you, he …)
- **possessive adjectives** (Possessivbegleiter; my, your, his …)

1 Family

- **auxiliaries to have, to be** (Hilfsverben)
- **comparisons with -er / -est** (Steigerung)
- **constructions with comparisons** (Satzbau bei Vergleichen; (not) as … as)

2 Friends

- **auxiliaries have / has got, can / can't** (Hilfsverben)
- **constructions with there + be** (Satzbau)

3 Home town

- **present simple** (einfache Gegenwart)
- **adverbs of frequency** (Häufigkeitsadverbien; always, often …)
- **possessive pronouns, object form** (Personalpronomen in Objektform; me, you, him …)

4 Pets and animals

- **ordinals** (Ordnungszahlen; 1st - 31st)

5 Birthdays

- **present progressive** (Verlaufsform der Gegenwart)

6 Shopping and …

- **auxiliaries must, should, have to** (modale Hilfsverben)

7 School

- **questions and negative answers with do, don't** (Frage und Verneinung)

8 Free time

- **past simple** (einfache Vergangenheit)

9 Holidays

Spielerisch Fremdsprachen lernen

... mit weiteren Sprach-
büchern aus dem Verlag
ars≡dition!

Hier eine Auswahl:

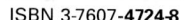

ISBN 3-7607-**4724-8**   ISBN 3-7607-**4725-6**

ISBN 3-7607-**4719-1**   ISBN 3-7607-**4720-5**
Tonkassette -**4748-5**   Tonkassette -**4749-3**